AF374238

After Þwelling on Earth

After Dwelling on Earth

Reflections at 84

PETER WELTNER

marrowstone press

Table of Contents

PART 1

Guanyin

Mournful eyes leave nothing for my sight to
yield to but the sorrow you left
behind. I wait for you
as in a mirror looking upon terror, bereft
of my senses, not your light
but only your shadows reawakening
me to another departure. Fireflies, bright
and golden, flicker at twilight like lanterns being
borne high over their shoulders
by mourners
on their way to the shrine
of the Goddess of Mercy, the ever smiling,
ever silent one, the ceremonial line
of them so beautifully paced and right
it appears to be celebratory, as grief must be sometimes,
my love.

Enlightenment

I mourn for my lost friends,
rivers, forests, the ocean
I live by, whatever rends
the heart, the heedless motion
of futurity. Strong, steady
winds sift sand through sea
oats, ice plants. Marin's hills
are misted blue. Self-pity
is to see oneself in others' ills.
A crow pecks at a sea bass'
carcass until it's bloodied
the sand. I am the same as
fish heads, crab shells, a rat
decaying in swaying dune grass.
I am compassion. I am this. I am that.

Blind Man at the Gate

Guided, never alone, hiking on rocky, dusty
trails, crossing turbulent rivers, over
cloudless deserts, thirsty, hungry,
trying to reach the border,
to bear witness, give testimony
to a people's suffering years after
the coup, to seek solace, peace
after wandering through wilderness,
praying as he would at an altar,
or under the sorrowful eyes of Jesus
in a splintering icon of Veronica's veil
that his fate no more be desolate, life fail
him no more, that the gift of a beneficent vision be given
him, not to see but be seen by the grace of what happens.

Suicide

Two brawny men stand on a promontory
by a stormy sea at continent's end
as a tall thin boy paces anxiously
near where the empty beach bends
toward cliffs. He wades into waves
surging high enough to wash over
him in a tidal rush toward caves,
turns, sees the two staring. The water
is icy, aching. He plunges deeper
in, leaps out of it, then lets himself go.
Like a castle's sentinels, tower's guardsmen,
the watchers, dispassionate, careful, slow
to make judgments, hesitate. The sun sets,
full of regrets, though it disbelieves in sin,
understanding of the need for departure as it's always been.

The Penitent

Its feathers black as a cassock, a fat raven
pecks at driftwood, struts on the seawall.
Long misty clouds, like contrails, linen
white, fade away, yesterday's squalls
over for a while. In the park, wild roses',
poppies', sorrel petals open wide
to morning, to what the sun proposes
for the coming day. It is now low tide.
Might wrongs be cleansed by purging
lives the way storms seize wave after
wave to crash against beach, boulders,
cliffs? I think of us then, in the deepening
night, through the waves' crests' thundering,
listening to a seabird's crying, high and piping, I, I, I.

Easter Morning

Daybreak, there's no human, no mortal sound.
At night, I see you going further away. Winter's
snow's melted. I look everywhere around
the house You're not here, no longer
part of me. I've spent my life vainly.
Time passes by us exceedingly
swift. I feel like a ghost adrift
to nowhere, a shadow dying from
early morning's excesses. Try to sift
water from water, air from breezes,
light from light, one passion from another.
The tides have nothing to teach us, ordered
by the moon to rise and fall. You left me
too soon to love me. I want you to come
back. Let us walk on the beach so spiritually we leave no traces.

An Ancient Silk Screen in the Asian Museum

North, south of the serpentine river, snow
is melting. It's early spring Will it rain
on the peasants' new-dug graves tomorrow?
Under a rocky, treeless mountain's
shadows, monks pray to what has brought
lives here where vines entangle a cave
lost spirits hide in, those who'd sought,
while able to, the solace of grace, pine,
maple, and oak, ivy, an eagle's opulent
wings at sunset, bearing torches that save
men from dragons while on the far right a line
of calligraphy is swooping down like heaven-sent
feathers falling out of the sky, like wisps of silent
souls flying back to an earth without pain or sorrow, where old
gray men, in sight of the moon, pour from jugs more rice wine.

Ishmael

Unshielded from danger, hiking on rocky, dusty
trails, crossing streams, rivers, over
random paths, through deserts, thirsty,
hungry, lost in a world without order,
unable to offer any testimony
to God, a wanderer
cast out by Him, he builds an altar
not to kneel before it, his spirit grasping after
nothing from the past, but a site to pray to a star,
perhaps, or to the earth's halting breaths, the skies'
widening firmaments or maybe even
to Hagar, his vanished mother, who in having given
him birth had given him her grief, another forever
outsider lost in a wilderness not of their making
but their destiny nonetheless, worthy of prayer, having to journey
aways dressed shabbily in endless mourning, sackcloth and ash, day after day.

Horace on His Critics

After Epode 6

Why lambast me, you tail-wagging mutts,
you sniveling curs. You should be
afraid of wolves, foxes like me.
Who barks, snaps, howls, ruts
as weakly as you? You're pathetic,
you snarling, weaselly critics,
ears pricked up as I bound
through woods after you,
waiting for you to go to ground.
You old strays. You defamed me.
Nothing you write or say is true.
And I? I'm a bull with massive horns
ready to gore you for your dishonesty,
blaming Rome's ills on me and my poetry.

Remember how Archilochus, when denied
his beautiful, young daughter's hand,
by Lycambes, wrote a poem so injurious
about him it drove the man to suicide?
Or Hippomax, who wrote such vile
words about the sculptures
of Bupalo that he took chisel to tile
and graffitied on Rome's walls that black
lagoon creature's massive flaccid cock
and labeled it, "Impotent Hippo's." Attack
me no more or you will hear the like
from me, you churlish beasts. I'll destroy
you like a boy rakish with his magic marker for the joy
of it, besting his bullies with two or three words and a flick of his hand.

The Logic of Remus' Murder

After Horace, Epode 7

Where are you, Romulus, forcing us to go
now, back to more foreign wars, swords
unsheathed, greedy, rabid for death? Who
made you tell ancient lies, whose words
taunted you to force us to burn grain, set fire
to fields, houses, imperil seas, cross plains,
kill so many? To capture children, enchain
men, women, murder those who aspire
too high, to march foes down the Sacred
Way in shame, turn soldiers into slaves? Lions,
leopards don't slaughter their own kind. We've fed
on our brothers' flesh, we noble, impure Romans.
Fratricide is our history. Spare us its lust for violence,
cursed as we are by those we've butchered for their innocence.

Sinbad

Feverish desire impels you to where he curls
in bed like a restless purring cat,
rustling sheets as he twirls
his hair, bites his nails, lying flat
on his back, having prayed for the sea's
currents, breezes to sail you over
stormy waters to him, you like bees
to flowers, he says of you, the voyager
crossing seas wind-borne like them to hive
and honey. His body yields to yours upon
his, sunlit-golden, while you taste his nectar on
your lips, the pomegranate, oranges, lemons that thrive
in searing heat, attar, passion flowers, the heady wine
he pours from his chalice to salute you, sweet as grapes
from his gated garden.

There's Always a Lake in This Story

Mallards sleepily drifting. A waxing
moon under white sheets
of clouds.
A dam overflowing
into a creek.
Winds rustling through long-leaf
pine, oak, hickory. A grief
apart enshrouds
lost lives in dreams. The hot, humid air.
A car door slammed, footsteps
on dry sand. What only the young dare
do. Two bodies blossoming by spring's precepts
into burgeoning passions. Bliss
to be innocent. The lake's lapping waters. The first kiss.

Red

Last night, over untilled fields, a red moon
burned so hot it burst into flames
like molten steel, fat as a red balloon,
a child's, tied to a string. The same
red as a cartoon heart, the flush red
of shame, embers, roses, poppies
as glossy scarlet dresses, autumn apples,
lightning flashes, rainbows, of lips new wed
to lipstick kisses. Bruises. Blushing faces.
Christmas candle wax. Icons' rubies. The red
of blood gushing from deep wounds, dead
men's scars, enflamed gums, blood-shot
eyes, of fear, bursting stars, spilled guts.
The blistering red of festering terrors, the sun
rising to burn the world to annihilation. Ecstasy. Volcanic passion.

Red and Blue

Red as wine drunk from fluted
glasses, embers smoldering
in burned-
out forests, caterpillars'
scarlet eyes, sweat tasting
of hot metal, cars'
exhausts, memories
of thwarted passions.

Blue as regrets lost
in shadows
twisting across
winter hills, as ice crevices
in love's wintry seasons,
blue as a bluesman, you by night glow.

Town House on East 71st

Jasmine, magnolia, amethysts, roses
shown in sharp focus, life
up close, scissors, knife,
crystal bowls, Chinese vases,
wide curtained windows
the sun stares through
dispassionately, the shadows
it forms of you not knowing what to do,
silhouetted on walls
as you pace the carpet
in this movie overloaded with stop motion
stills while snow-flake-like lily petals
drift onto the bloodied floor restored in the film's set
by the camera as it pans past candelabra, petits gateaux,
gold-trimmed porcelain.

Old Friends

After Horace, Odes 2.14

Old age comes, our wrinkles multiple, so what?
Why rage against it?
Sacrifice ten, twelve oxen. A lot
of good that'll do. Throw a fit.
Who cares? The gods are unappeasable.
Let's drink
our fill, not overthink
our lives We're incapable
of wisdom. South Winds spread
diseases haphazardly. The dead
dwell among us to remind us
of how grass covers
us all, sooner or later,
all of us superfluous.

The river Cocytus, or one of its
tributaries, will carry
us there. "I'm at wit's
end with fear," you cry out to me.
You've planted, watered,
pruned, watched
rose bushes thrive.
More's the pity
they'll survive
you. You've stored wine for better
times in your cellar,
haven't you? Here's a mirror
for you, Marcus. Look, every line
in your face's like mine, is ominous as mine. Let's get drunk.

The Indifferent One

Your eyes were haunted like a child's, a drifter,
your face shadowed by fear
of growing older
lest your beauty, so dear
to you, should be taken from you: at my door,
I begged you to stay,
to make love with me
again, your smile so kind as you walked away
I thought I saw, ever so slightly,
an indifference to life
grown tragic, aristocratic, some might say,
in its pride and nobility, like an inner strife
between you and the universe, your soft red lips,
kind as your finger tips
on my body, rounded into a kiss, your face masked like an actor's.

Tossed Stones

It's mid-spring. Honeysuckle, thornless wild roses
bask in the sun. It's still chilly at dawn. I'd say
we were born in shadows, among trees
like these, learning to roam, how to play
in half light, under canopy. I dreamt of us
last night. Spiky rusted spruce needles.
Sappy milkweed. Wind-bent tiger lilies.
the stones we'd toss into creeks. The moss.
Today, the sun waits to rise like a pale thin disc
on a craggy, spruce-lined horizon. I say, "I don't want
this, us, me and you, anymore. I can't risk
it, our needing to hide in woods each time." I pant
like a dog after I've said it. You take my hand
in yours. It's late April again. Always, this way, you understand.

A Gardener

After Stevens

He's a haltering, frail caretaker of a garden
numbering the days until spring flowers
blossom again, like many old men,
women mocked by how hours
pass by them so quickly,
forgetful as they are, memory
not what it used to be. There's a river
near his cottage, steady, tranquil,
the sea-seeking source of lost dreams,
flowing wherever its banks will
take them, like a stream that's the bearer
of past things. Let be be beginning of seems,
and he, once more, lovingly tucked under covers,
falling asleep to scents of hyacinths, lilacs, nasturtiums.

River Ice

For Gerald Coble

The rising sun says to me, "Come, come
with me." And so I go, follow
it, letting it show me my way home.
Scattered patches of late snow
blanket last year's leaves.
I rest in the mammoth shadow
of an ancient oak that perceives
me as I must be now. Teals, geese calls
reawaken sleepy lakes. Larches'
needles look rusty after last fall's
lightning, slivers of ice dripping off branches.
Reeds catch dawn's breezes in their twitchy
trembling fingers as the sun gently guides me
to the river's thin sheer sheets of still icy water,
its moon-softened light glowing like a ghost's misty
face in a mirror.

Departure at the Crossroads

Our lives are nearly over. The night is silent.
save as I listen to midnight's ghosts,
the distant sibilance of waves sent
like messages from the dark to lost
souls. I remember how the anguish
of spring meant everything to you,
cranes crying over a shrine like a wish
to be immortal, like the pale azure
noble sash you wore wrapped too
tightly round your waist to assure
strangers of your beauty, your silken skin
sleek, sheer as golden brocade. Daringly thin
clouds embrace the sun. In the east, a taut wind gathers
where men worship gods. We must part. Our love is all that matters.

Beach Balls

A beach ball drifts away with tides
washing beaches'
scattered shells
as a surfer rides
waves, the sea's
sudden swells
limitless
on a joyous day
turned inglorious,
the way children learn to play
on sand by being teased
or teasing others, until suddenly seized,
at water's edge, by fear of the infinite,
the greedy sea, the meaningless loss of a toy.

Haze

An autumn sun in late summer,
leaves falling
from trees early, brittle, sly,
unpredictable, blazing
hot afternoons, the sky
yielding none of its space
back. Lightning without thunder.
A cloud absentmindedly
slides east. There's no shade, no place
for relief, no succor or refuge. Try
to speak of better
times than these, nights too blistering
to sleep in, to speak of, the black sky, pulsing stars
seeing better than we see the iron-gray smoke that's ours
and our wars.

Fog at Dusk

A pale sun, subdued by mist, sinks
below a frail horizon. I've studied
fog all my life. Who thinks
of crows and gulls gathered
together on the gray wall
of a promenade as a sign
of holier matters, the call
of white waves cresting, birds
resting on a tidal barrier, as matters
of design? Winds blow sandy-
yellow sea-froth like petals willy-nilly
over the strand, like freely strewn blessings,
as high tide and fog slowly occupy the beach
hide it under dew and drizzle, with nothing to teach
us but this: how fog and dusk commune with night to claim us all.

Asilomar Waves

Imagine this black and white photo shows the cliffs
of a lone small island incapable
of resistance against stiff
winds, fierce currents, a fabled
place rapacious seas surround—
itself peaceful, edenic. Then, one day,
it explodes. Think Thera. Think
Krakatoa. All who drowned
in an eruption that can slay
thousands in an instant, the merest wink
of an eye. Then consider how a camera's capacity
to capture the roiling clouds of smoke darkening
skies, obscuring cliffs, ruins, bodies under debris
after it blows is really, here, an image of waves exploding
on a solitary boulder near to shore in a simulacrum of our destiny.

A Lone Cypress

For Nathan Wirth

An old man's been changed like Daphne—
whether for or by the sun who knows?—
into a wind-weathered tree,
rooted in rock, bony limbed,
craggy, solitary, the blows
of age having bent it, twisted
it into a witch-. hag-like monstrosity,
prophetic, ominous, a guard,
a sentinel on a boulder-tower,
keeping watch over the sea,
placid, quiet now, for now unharmed
by Pacific storms, safe, its innocence
like a joy in living the Old Cypress
knows not to betray, to keep his silence,
a man-tree weathered, unfelled, bearing witness.

Redwoods

For Lydia Wirth

The moon's reflection on the Russian River
courses its steady journey, fluent as
ghosts, its pale light by force of water
broken into bits and pieces, life as it was
rippling, silvery as fish scales under the sun
by day, shining gem-like as stars at night,
your eyes sparkling, too, as we walk, my friend,
toward dusk as it might be were it held as tight
against death as our arms hold each other,
having arrived at path's end, to that bend
in the river that leads to a forest to wander
in forever, without ever talking or needing to,
in wonder at how calmly they're being left behind,
those years we've been together, hoping to find,
in night's hushed darkening, the words for what woods say and do.

PART II

Dwelling on Earth

Renderings after Heidegger

1. Horace, after Epistle 2.1

Like thought, poetry must be rooted in the earth.
You who choose to praise notorious barbarian
tyrants, repressive states, men worth
nothing, warrior cults, mighty Parthian

forts built to protect them from other's
ways of thinking than theirs, what music
do you hear in woods, valleys, rivers
but your own martial measures, epic's

drumbeats to war? I wish all wars were over.
I fought in one, you know, not Gallipoli,
Saipan, Vietnam, Ukraine, but Philippi
on Brutus's behalf, and, frightened, ran away.

I'd chosen the better, yet losing side. May
Janus, the two-faced hypocrite god, close
the gates he's guarded so weakly these years
of civil wars, conquests, humanity's silenced tears.

I hope I possess too much self-knowledge to write
epic nonsense. I'd despise being acclaimed
as a poet who'd praised bloodshed, scribbled
panegyrics to warlords, as if my sense of sight,

of right and wrong had died in the victory
of a blood-soaked ruler. For this truth is
what life grimly assures us of: we'll all be
borne off some day by those who miss

us to our graves in plain wooden closed coffins,
passing through streets that stink of shit, piss
cheap sweet perfumes, burning incense, trash bins,
peppers, spices, and whatever other odoriferous

products wrapped in waste paper we use to deny
the stench of death, all of us extinguished like light
in night's totalitarian kingdom. Do not despair. The glory
of life is the earth's gift, the words that speak of us

and the world as one. If living's to receive the praise
it craves, it must be written down or else forgotten.
These are the deeds of language for each of our days:
the knowledge of joy as the poetry of absented things, left unspoken.

2. Horace, after Odes 2.3

Be mindful of tomorrow's sorrows, my friends.
Never rejoice in today's gainful successes.
Whether you're sad or happy mends
nothing. The whims of time curse, bless

us as they will. Let yourself be embraced by
friends, family, lovers, not by the greedy
hands of chance. Drink wine, if you care
to, find pleasures where you can. No pine

or poplar grows tall to shade you, no pear
or apple grows ripe for you to taste it, no wine
knows your name as you drink it. A rippling
stream's a fine place to make love by

or a covert of leafy oaks. Smell blossoming
flowers' enticing lovely perfumes. Try
to enjoy youth for the brief time it lasts.
Someone's always urging us to go this way,

that. Everyone stands fatherless under
one sky. Everyone follows Orcus' orders,
downward. What more is there to say?
When fate's urn breaks, your lot's been

determined. We live between the seen
and the unseen. Call that the border
between the world and poetry, the river
we sail on to be exiled in darkness forever,

fluent as time. I cultivate words like fields
of grain, with hoe, plow, oxen, rake,
sickle. Spring rains fall. Summer sun yields
golden wheat, these seeds my poems are, for art's sake.

3. *Josef von Eichendorff, after Der Umkehrende (4)*

Whatever life looks upon is endlessly
changing, day as it dies turning
blood red, joy not what it seems to be
but the hidden horror of death in everything.

Sorrow, pain come like thieves in
the night, stealthily, pacing floor
boards silently, like a love you win
by leaving it, bidding goodbye, closing the door.

Someone must cleanse the earth better,
release its tenants of their misery,
for why should any new soul suffer
being born in a place without mercy?

Let charity, poetry break free, fall from
heaven upon everything we
build or make or do. Let us see
the sky again by it and call it our welcoming home.

The Messenger

For Robert Mohr

1.

In the noon-heightened brilliance of Santa Monica,
everything looks white, streets, bushes, grass,
orange tiles, red bricks. Imagine an Alhambra
white marble light cast on things as they pass
into mirages, a blue white sky, its blinding
clarity like strips of crepe paper from yesterday's
parade, purple, ruby, chartreuse bleaching
in the heat, or waves gushing, crashing the ways
they hide the sea, beach in mist, like veiled
apparitions, as I walk on a long crowded pier by
the Pacific, sensing uncertainly how my life has failed
others even as a girl stretches a white scarf against the sky,

like a sheet of ice, to see it more clearly by while behind
her a line of guys, their trousers black, baggy,
their shoes shiny, t-shirts white, tight, beautifully
sweaty, smoke hits of weed. Why do they remind
me of the little church I visited once in Laguna,
the late afternoon sun, through its honey-colored
windows, falling onto its scrubbed plaster walls,
seeping into the white of them like a light offered
to God, His impenetrable absence, as if He calls
to us to be stripped of colors in the purity of his Being,
drenched in white, its emptiness like a last illusion as if As
were all He'd ever meant for His people to be free of, as that, as this—

say, as white as glory on a beautiful day welcoming
us to it, even though it must, faster than us, pass
away. Back outside, I hiked down a cliff, fat,
thick with long-lived rosy succulents, the strand
empty, the sand hot, gritty, as I paced waiting
for night, for the black kindness of darkness
to tell me of what I try to, yet cannot understand.
The sky was blank, yet luminous, the horizon a silvery
gray, the cliff behind me a maroon so deep
it was radiant. Twilight reddened, thinned, faded then quickly
vanished to nothing while I searched for a cave to sleep
in. A craggy boulder was wisely spying on me, a seal barking

at the waves. The beach at night is always a solemn place,
at a solemn hour. Fog drifted in—gauzy, pallid, hovering
over the shore, its shroud clothing earth with grace,
like God's face, maybe, hiding behind its nightly
veil. Waves, breaking, turned white, solid as alabaster
under moonlight seeping through mist, like sculpted water,
as here where the sun's abandoning Santa Monica's hills.
Azaleas, passion flowers, bougainvillea, daffodils,
fuchsias close their eyes in rows in the gardens
behind me, the scotch broom, the bright lemons,
the dusky fennel too abundant, too dazzling to look
at one by one, too ravishing even at night, too youthful to be borne

in such profligacy, like an excess of words in a book
to read or too many pictures in a gallery to be seen.
On the beach, watching the sunset, I'm waiting for
peace, I suppose, the fog to roll back in, the white light
of night to come with its own luminosity to restore
light to the blank screen that's a life about to begin or after
it's just ended, like riding a wave, an old surfer
once told me, the joy he felt past all that's fit or right,
like being briefly poised between worlds, between motion
and stillness, dusk, dawn, like lives lived twice over in memory
at its keenest, in an instant glimpsing sky and beach and ocean
as if they were all one being in the elation, and folly, of a cosmic unity.

2.

A high tide is sweeping the beach,
the wide strand white as snow
with wind-swept froth, the foggy sky bleach
white, the white water slow
to roll in, but visible far as the Farallons.
The dunes' sea oats blow in the winds,
the seals on rocks sleeping like a cartoon's
seals flopping on couches. So the day begins,
white and still and happy as the sun rises
over the eastern hills, nothing yet invisible
in a morning's light's particularly intense clarities,
each thing seen, for a moment, in its barest reality, tree, rock,
runner, surfer, gull, crow.

We know no more than what we see
and feel. The eye of a raven gazes at me
where it perches on the wall
of the promenade, inquisitively,
I suppose. Ignoring the call
of its owner, a dog barks at waves.
Blue anemones flower in the pools of caves
nearby. What I mean to say is what saves
us from ourselves might be the invisibility
hidden within what we do see, however inattentively,
the way the words in poetry, literature, might be variations
on the depths of things like a world elusively spoken of, nobly,
in dawn's infinite interpretations.

Plague Years by the Russian River

Plovers run for cover from the wild inrushing
tides, calling his name as I, thinking of injustice,
make a pillow out of a rock, not knowing
where he might be waiting for me, lice
in my hair, fleas in my jeans, tide pools
cliffside not sensing where to flow to.
What idiots poets are, what errant fools.
They say, Look. Sun. Moon. Awestruck.
Make of them deities. The winds that blow
as clouds scatter. He and I pull oars, out of luck,
our boat going wherever the river takes it.
When I think of him tomorrow, will I remember
his pain best? Or the cliff edge where we'd sit
staring at churning water, water, waste and water?

Do all poets write poems to lie to themselves?
How can they deny the way the world
works if not by falsifying what a tree tells
us about how we live. I see him now curled
in our bed, with nothing to give him, nothing
to leave him with as I try to lift him by
his armpits, bone-weakened by his suffering,
the days after too lonely, desolate to cry
for him, hoping for more dark, silence till dawn.
Not even the mountain trails I hike on
feel alive now, not even the great birds
of the mountains. Rain, more rain, useless words.
I walk home and look at our deadened room as he
turns away from me, as if to escape me into the final agony.

If we had spanned the Russian River with a dam
to contain it, the water would flow in constant
peace, never flooding. If I could name one name
to give it, it would be his. That is all I want.
This is all I wish for. Fantasies. Impossibilities.
A stone bridge spans upper shallows, but ceases
to be when the river overflows into alluvial weeds.
Or a log bridge that withers and sprouts no more.
it's late fall and very cold   No one I know reads
of those days now. They're done, over. Only the floor
of a redwood forest shows me myself as I
am today in the years since his absence. All I've written
means nothing, the woods' silence too fearsome to try
to speak of, like wild fires' feverish haze left in clear air forgotten.

We unhappy travelers lie down to sleep and cannot sleep,
recollecting the past. It's frightening to allow
the mind its awful freedom. Dreadful the deep
dark nights of dreams struggling to follow
eyes into their re-waking to earth. There were taller trees
before, where I'd found him. There was a summer
once that'd govern our lives, green leaves
and mossy green spiky needles in the tangled order
of wilderness and river, whirlwind and whirlpool
and rippling waves, a moon sailing through rifts
in clouds to lift our spirits. How easy it is to fool
ourselves into trusting nature's voices, gulls flying high over
dusk-gray boulders by the river's mouth as a stormy wind shifts
sand among straying dunes while the sun dives into itself and shatters.

A New Ode to an Old Dionysos

For Atticus Carr

The phallic hymns, sung in processions
With flutes and tambourines, must honor
The God Dionysus, for all the nighttime
Oracular frenzy would be profane if not
To celebrate a God.
David Plante, "The Death of a Greek Lover"

1. Strophe

Hoary wind-blown olive trees, their thick trunks
gnarled, knobby, limbs twisted into knots—
yet their fruit's juicy, pungent, the flesh
luscious eaten soon after its fallen to earth.
Thornless wild roses bask in the sun. It's
still cold at dawn. Who tests a fire to see if it
burns but a child? Yet we light a torch at
his feast to guide us to his seaside cave,
crying, bearing ivy, olive leaves, dew-
fresh and silvery, propitiatory gifts to the deity
who demands these rites from us who are
his devotees, thirsty for old joys, offering wine,
cheeses, roasted lamb, jars of winnowed grain,
the marble vessels we bring, too, lovely thistles,

redolent roses worn in our hair as we chant
in his grove happily, giddily, even we elderly
ones, as if by dancing we revive our youth,
long over, feverish, struck by sudden
rushes of blood, our breaths quickening to
a runner's pace, the finishing line in sight,

like victors who will be celebrated, garlanded
in violets, daffodils tossed onto our sweating
bodies here, now, as we celebrate our god's
ways as day's last light falls upon us, our voices
rising to sing this song wreathed as we are
in the folly of the Muses, we withered Bacchae,
wrinkled, bewhiskered, and weathered, skinny
as cattails, gaunt as milkweed, who sing inharmoniously.

2. *Antistrophe*

The western sky blazes a fiery red
at last light, the sky burning
brightest where it's bled
through veils of clouds. Flying
toward grassless hills, pelicans' wings
are tipped in yellow and gold
like angels' feathers in icons. It is
an unsettling sunset we see,
like a passion fading
into dusky, gritty gray,
like a last, swift kiss
before we silently let
ourselves return to sleep, a dark day
ahead and we, confusingly, death-bound, frighteningly old.

And so soon we will fall asleep, waiting for
another dawn, the uncertainty
of each morning, the ardor
we knew yesterday secretly
slipping away, as if without mercy,
while tomorrow's sun, blurred, lazy,
and fat, promises no more. A hungry eyed crow's
perched on a wire
like a creature
that knows
as long as the earth endures
its kind shall soar freely. Priapus, you have given
us wings to fly with. Let your vows not be forgotten,
talismans against evil, bearers of gifts, the flights of desire.

3. Epode

To where will we fly, if not to woodland lakes,
pools, ponds below thunderous cascades
in hickory, maple, rhododendron forests, rivers
slithering lazily through corn fields like snakes,
beaches off wide strands whose depths a man wades
into, testing the waters up to his waist, never shivers,
not even in winters, warmed by a sun delighting
in his beauty as it does all those on beaches on holidays,
pressing flesh against sweating flesh, spirits flourishing
in the heat and the beats of a music that stays
in the mind like paeans to bodies near water? A creek trickling
at night in the thick of timberland might be where you go

again to meet him as his note said you should in the safety
of woods, moonlight better than sunshine any day for making
love: all these liquid, earthy places for passion we know
of, sing of, the gymnasium reliving the glory
days of Greece, shower rooms, saunas, hot tubs,
dance floors, after theater parties, crowded bars,
beachside cliffs which gave us in our youth
shadows to cruise in, or by piers, docks, back rooms in clubs,
cheap motels, barn haylofts, back seats of cars,
each in pursuit of pleasure, an ancient god's truth
the knowledge of which induces souls to imagine heaven
is passion's ambition. Let us pray, though its too late for us to
return to those lost days, that we remember, even if dreamily,
how the sun, early, maybe too bright, would shine on us to awaken
us to moments of joy. Oh, Dionysos: no one honors you when you
fail them. Rise. Restore your ancient powers. Be mindful of your bounty.

4. And Turn

Still higher we soared
as marvels poured
over us, inspiriting our souls,
having no goals

but to touch each other, to reach
beyond ourselves, failing each
time to do so, recoiling from glory,
its incommensurable immensity

too painful to behold—death,
life scrolls to be read prayerfully
with each breath,
like poems exhorted

for eternal meanings. See how
my friends stare sadly down at me
beyond the sights of the living? Show,
me how to love you as you love me, seeking no other.

Honeysuckle, immortal wild roses
unfold to the sun at dawn. Whose
pasts are these, lives hiding in shadows
like a vision of old sorrows

transfigured by pleasure? Like specks of dust
floating in the air, misty
leaves sparkling with winter's rust,
a pond on whose swarthy

banks reeds, cattails, milkweed,
tiger lilies thrive in the same morning sun
burning through our window: so you lie next to me
out of old men's need

to declare their love for each other,
as if forever
unknowing what a life together
has meant; as if, every day, it's just begun,

that communion
between us of an understanding
not even we can grasp, hold onto,
we venerable singers

in an antique, dissonant, feeble chorus,
chanting and dancing
to earth and air and water
as if to Dionysos

with flutes and tambourines in a late-
life frenzy, maddened by
the reign of death, seeking to satiate
ourselves in the oldest, most sensual deity

we can sing to, he in his naked beauty,
more glorious than a newly risen
morning, more incarnate
than heaven.

Shifting Lines Bending Time

For Galen Garwood

I

1.

There's a river in time like a line tranquil,
steady, yet shifting, never still,
flowing toward a faraway sea
which after waking you'll see, sleepily,
is yours to float on—its waves like a tidal
current on which you drift like a leaf, a petal.

2.

Jasmine, magnolia, gardenia, honeysuckle,
roses, ivy formed by the golden
light of a full moon, a beacon
guiding you, shining on your garden
so lovingly its timeless mystery
appears more beautiful for its ephemerality.

3.

The scarlet eyes of cater-
pillars is the red of sunset on winter
hills, molten metal,
pink abalone shells,
passion's rubies, regrets
like that, whoever forgets them.

4.

Mallards, gliding. Herons, fishing. Flickering
stars sparkling on a lake. A dam overflowing
into a creek. Grasses blowing in rustling
winds. Tires on asphalt. A car door
slammed. In the hot, humid air, you're
enfolding me in time as it rushes by, weeping, sweating.

5.

An autumn sun's reminiscent of summer,
a few late leaves slipping into a river
as black clouds gather and slide east
to where a darkening sky's beginning
to flower with winter's soon-to-be feast
of clear nights' stars perennially re-blooming.

6.

A seabird soars, feathering
its wings, pivoting,
dipping, circling,
skimming the sea,
displaying its beauty
proudly, like a lover risking everything.

7.

Wait as a boat in dry dock waits.
Be patient. Calm. Meditate.
The Pacific's much too stormy

tonight to walk beside safely.
Isn't it for art's sake we stay
awake: to watch stars turn into sea spray?

8.

You're a rose blooming far lovelier
than any flowers bloom,
your body unfurling in my bedroom
more openly than any
rooted thing is able to, you so sensually
alive to the hour, carnal as a metaphor.

9.

Go. Leave now. I've been wanting
to tell you of the risk, to quit you soon.
Erotic itches, sexual longings,
sweltering ecstasy, Dionysian
swooning, both of us suspended in
the oblivion of too rapturously being no one.

10.

November cold grips the day as furrow-
browed clouds with glum clown faces
hover weightily over oaks, spruces,
long-leaf and pitch pines. Below
the tree line, night waits for us with its silences,
its intimations of winter woods smothered under snow.

11.

You were the best of men, my friend,
who gazed upon monsters swimming
in the oceanic depths of your soul,
eager to swallow you, to end
your days in despair, always dreading
drowning in terror of the one good true and beautiful.

12.

Why waste time enflaming cities with wars?
Sleep and let the sea sleep
and rocks and stones and trees sleep
even in spring. Think of the stars,
how they, too, despair and weep
for the world they knew and could not keep.

II

1.

What are these winds ruining swallows' wings,
Li Shangyin asked, violating
their flights, the moon avowing
no sister, no brother,
time's powers
limitless, yet ever changing?

What fate has led him to flee
worlds where burning
flowers in their beauty
stood in for candles, lighting
his way to see
earth better by?

Winnowed wheat yields tares,
not seeds to feed
us. Does time ever change
life's bitterness to please
us, arrange
it to lead

us to happiness, visions of jade
rooms, pearl lined palaces?
What exile has led
him to places where he's laid
his head yet wakes each morning
to a light that's said

to be sadder than rain at dawn-break,
the road he's traveled on
bewildering, under an old sky's iron-
gray cage and sunlessness on a lake
northern geese, mandarin ducks no longer
rest on, drifting, afraid of hunters, hungry soldiers.

2.

And an exiled Chu Yuan lamented he dwelled
in a forest where daylight
never meets its
shadows, filled
with a mist like night's
blowing in clouds, wet

and heavy until rain falls drowning
memories of home where he's gathering
larkspur that grew on
the hillside into his arms
to cradle like a child, the mountain
spring he drank from, no harms

to fear from its woods, listening
to thunder, lonely
and sleepy,
his spirit blown mid chaos,
boulder and hyacinth despairing,
too, of the loss

that has made him into an outcast,
spares him no joyful thoughts
as he waits at noon
under the shade of cypresses
brooding on what lasts
and what's too soon

gone, longing for the sun's glare to warm him
from what time's wrought
upon him, imagining a singer
with a lute grieving with him for the home
he's been exiled from,
thrown into a world formless and random.

III

You've left. The stars have changed.
Where is the line between
life and death, the challenged
space no one's known or seen?
The wine's been drunk, the rice eaten,
the air mingling the odors of beeswax and cinnamon.

I use old photographs as bookmarks,
read into the night to the music
of cicadas and moths like sparks
fizzing, buzzing by my window, the antic
hooting of owls. The moon
I shout to cannot hear me. Too late begun,

my days of spring, of youthful fervor.
Fireflies light the withered
grasses. Leaves droop as if ardor
were a matter of failure, embittered
things clinging to the end of time,
stooped, bent like a sign

meant to be read, then abandoned as illegible.
My heart grows sore listening to midnight,
yet how seductive, beautiful
music is when heard between twilight
and dawn, as if my shrouded body
were unbinding itself into eternity.

You've seen how ghosts' breaths write
on mirrors, how their words no longer
belong to them but to us, like a rite
of passage we trace with a finger,
then wipe off the glass. Life belongs
to that wisp of inscription, its death-devoted songs.

You ask how long it will be before I return.
No date is set, all else uncertain.
Put a light in the window. I yearn
to see you. A line in poetry can be
like that, set in the dark, a flame burning
in a window out of love, hopeful, anticipatory.

Seven Needful Words

1. *Metanoia*

Those who know no fear cannot be just.
Impiety is to treat unkindly those who
are in need. Do not sharpen hatred
on the whetstone of bloodshed. Do not
incite a people to warfare. No longer
deify vengeance, but sanctify peace.
Kindness springs from the earth. Breathe
its bracing air, drink from its rivers' clear
spring waters and be freed from thirst and grief.

Let love's new gods defeat the old ones' rages,
insisting ancestral crimes be revenged.
Let innocent words guide men's tongues
to a victory of the good. Let torches flare
and dance in Theseus' land and show the way
to hopefulness, women dressed in purple robes
men in white chitons banded together in song:
"Go, you children of night, you ancient, childless children,
you Furies, into death's caverns while you bless us in departure."

   After Aeschylus

2. *Forgiveness*

Submit to his absence the way water ripples in idle
gusts of wind, seaweed yields to a bay's tides.
Pursue him by dreamed of paths, never
resting, till you glimpse him as in real life,
the world you imagine the one you wake
to. How miserable it is to be ever hiding

from others' eyes. Your love will change
in a rain of tears when his face blossoms like
May in your heart, yet still you'll feel forgotten.
Life grows wretched, breaks the body, drifts
away like a sputtering candle. Forgive him for leaving.
It was his way of staying inside you, like the beauty
of flowers, hazy rains falling upon green fields by woods
where you stand, entranced, by warblers' singing to you as to everything.
 After Ono No Komachi

3. Compassion

The wind, sighing, retreats from the stinging stench of death
in the air. The sun, grieving, hides from its burden of sight.
In this place, it's hard to speak, to cry, to take a breath
that is not painful. The sky is dark, yet cruelly bright.
The young for the old, a poet wrote, that is tragedy.
Jesus. Persephone. Lear howling over his daughter,
Cordelia. But isn't it obscene to flee from death into story,
myth? A mother weeps, wonders why, receives no answer.
Another embraces her son against her breast, a boy killed
by a bomb that set their village on fire. Another waits
by her dying daughter's bedside. What evil has willed
it so? Yet another hesitates outside a door. Who hates
her son enough to execute him for no reason? And who is that there,
see?, from sorrow and loss rending her flesh, tearing her hair?
Wherever a child is suffering, in a city, town, on farmland, at sea,
or on a bone-laden barren hill, a mother stands grieving. Call her
Mary, but let her be whoever she is in her grief, ever nameless. Stabat Mater.
 After Jacopone da Todi

4. *Forsakenness*

My Lord, my Lord, why have you abandoned me?
You hear my words, how they roar against you
night and day, season after season. You are holy.
Yet you are silent. I am a worm, who never knew
you, unworthy. But why must I suffer so? People laugh
at me, scorn me, spit upon me. You gave me hope
at my mother's breast. Now I'm thistle and chaff.
Soldiers beat me with chains, scourge me with rope.
My blood's dried up, my body's broken like a potsherd.
When will you speak to me, when will I hear your Word?
I have been laid lower than the dust under the unsandled
feet of the lowliest of men, trampled on, defeated, crucified.
Where in my suffering shall I meet you? When will you greet
me among the desperate and lost, be brought to your promised land?

After Psalm 22

5. *Transfiguration*

Shortly after breakfast, he showed himself
by the sea of Tiberias and said to them,
"I am going fishing," and they followed,
climbed into the boat at night, but caught

nothing. At daybreak, he said, "You have
no fish to eat. Cast your net on the right side
of the boat." After they'd done so, his children
had caught so many they could not lift the net's

weight. And the one who'd been sleepily naked
put on clothes, leapt into the sea, and helped
the rest drag the nets filled with fish to shore
where a charcoal fire he'd prepared was used

to grill the catch which they ate with the bread
he'd given them, as a sign of their host's absence,
the last meal he'd blessed them with before leaving
them to be resurrected into life's ritual feasts of memory.

    After John 21

6. *Infinity*

All my long life I've worshiped a solitary hill,
lovely, empty, the way it hides the horizon
from my eyes, the dreamy genius, skill
it took to design it, the boundless suns
beyond it, infinitude, its resounding silence
deeper than mortal silences, its hushed peace
unfathomable, though I faced its presence
fearlessly, my heart quieted by its release
from sorrow. The wind moans, rushes rustle
through bushes with the voices of seasons
passing by us as my mind lets itself settle
into thoughts of eternity, seas we're wrecked in
with ease, blessed by the world's immensity as a way to begin
our voyage, drifting in eternal waters blissfully past mind's reach of
reasons.

    After Giacomo Leopardi

7. *Metamorphosis*

Two friends are staring at a large wide wall map.
A third is gazing, distracted, out a window.
Suppose its glass could be fitted, like a gap

between hills, over the map—call that tomorrow—
while the third still looks out it at the world.
But see? The other two know how to borrow

from metaphor. The third's become a bird hurled
out of the sky just from looking. Winds blow
him this way, that, like paper, like a bit of cartography

bending, crackling at the edges, like a page of poetry.
So the three agree, with no need for further discussion,
that creation must consist of an endless metamorphosis

of things, changing, transforming the world the way some music
converts the human spirit from tragedy into a vision
which sounds as God's laughter would sound transfigured into comic

art, Haydn's, Rossini's masses, say, how their pleas, eleisons, misereres
might evoke the sight of a man flying in the sky remapping land and
seas
just by looking out a window, astounded by heaven's painfully Ovidian
witty mysteries.

    After Yannis Ritsos

PART III

When Democracy Died Forever in Ancient Athens

after the Battle of Aegospotami (405 b.c.e.)

Youth's a wine jug fast emptied, drunk
to stupor, age a wine skin pitted
with life's dregs. When an oak trunk
is lightning-struck, it falls, uprooted.
When a ship in a gale wrecks on rocks,
it breaks apart. You drowned at
Aegospotami, Admantios. I lived,
but wander Athens in shame, defeated
as it is. I sit where you and I once sat
waiting for a play to start. Ours
were the dark days of furies, tragedies.
No matter how blue, how clear skies
are today, they offer no refuge. The city's
forsaken, beaten by Spartans, the clash of tyrannies.

All our once proud, decent men cower
before the enemy. Is that you or me
I see in a trance rising out of Hades?
Let me sleep as the sea sleeps
even if unknowingly, as stones, trees
sleep, and moon and stars. We
were more than friends, friend. I
drink my fill as a chill wind gusts
through me. You often said you'd die
first. Sea winds, a passionate sun
impel dozens of war-ready triremes on
whose decks we'd waited for the thrusts
and parries to start the fight. We were right, Admantios,
to fear for our lives. our final night of peace last seen in Pylos.

It's past time to leave life. The Dioscuri will guide
our boat over calm waters, gentle
winds hasten us forward, no more tied
to earth as we steer the oars bravely
on an unmapped journey, with no sure
destination, no city, no harbor as its
goal. What does it mean to abjure
the times we'd lived in when history sits
in its courts to judge us? What misty
fields are those we pass as cliffs'
boulders hurl broken rocks into the sea
while our storm-tossed boat safely drifts
onward, no one needing to row it anymore,
unburied shades greeting us along a crowded shore?

Look, by our docked boat, where waits the shade
of Megistias whom vicious Spartans killed
during the long days when they besieged
Amphipolis, threatening worse, more spilled
blood, more sword, spear carrying soldiers
wearing dented, bronze, visored helmets,
the town, as it fell, fated by what death sets
in stone forever, he a traitor intending to save
us, our city. Why is it a curse to betray
tyrants for a greater good? While he glowers
at you as if longing to confess to you, say
nothing to him. Your days, like his, are now winter
nights for which there are no words you might summon
to console him who stands with others never to be forgiven.

Must I return to the world of the unhappily living,
the fateful survivors of Aegospotami? I watch the sea
off Piraeus, old as the sun I'm praying
to, my youth meaning no more to me
than Apollo's cold, weary tears. It is a hot,
lazy afternoon. I walk beside empty
piers as a horned grebe flies over
pine trees, an olive grove. The flayed skin
of a goat dries like old clothes in the heat
of noon. It's the wonder of ruined things
that saddens me most, Athens turned traitor
while friends around us were dying, drowning
among swelling tides, burning ships, the suffering
all empires fall into, burning in its fires, drowning in its water.

And so I live alone in recollection, accomplishing
nothing, a stranger, no city, no refuge mine,
wandering, looking, remembering, watching
the losses I've known being wind-thrown,
like stone after stone, into the Aegean,
like dust blown randomly over the earth.
The last small battered shard I've saved
in my tunic's pocket I now hold in
my hand to show you where I've
chiseled crudely into it, as into
the fragment of a mast from a sinking
ship to be cast into the sea, to somewhere
unknown, bearing no message but my name, Petros,
and yours, Admantios, two warriors drowned together
the day Athens lost the war not to Sparta but its tyrannical self.

Virgil's Last Will, Revised

Adolebitque eam: and he will burn it

Anxious soothsayers read in birds' innards,
in blood bubbling up from wells, wolves
howling in Roman streets, tigers, leopards
escaped from cages, a star that revolves
against its orbit, lightning striking, burning
hay ricks, farmers' cottages under a sky
translucent as water: all this prophesying
frightened priests might achieve by
haruspication, augury, descrying the future
in scary phenomena, yet they'd failed
to predict Philippi's bloodshed, could assure
neither side of victory, nor warn those who wailed
in the aftermath, the farmers who with crooked
plows now daily turn up bones, spears, bloodied
swords rusting to nothing, an empty helmet, a graveyard.

Right and wrong alter roles with one another.
Wars abound throughout the world. It is hard
to know how many. War on the Rhine. War
on the Euphrates, in the Straits. Allied countries
violate their vows. Sword against sword.
Word against word. What god replies
to these blasphemies? The heavens are bored
with us. Horses break loose from tight reins
no longer gripped by charioteers. Who wins,
who loses in this chaos? Rome would have been
better if it had never been founded. The great sin
of my unfinished poem's to have inspired an empire,

to found an epic, heroic deed to be forever emulated. I tire
of it all, all this talk of greatness and power. Most of life
is pain. What does my poem like a priest predict? Eternal strife,

endless enmity, innumerable Caesars, one after
another, cruel and crueler. It would lave been
better for me to have stayed home, a farmer,
never to have written, than have turned flatterer.
Yes, most of life is sad. We may have seen
beautiful things, known some real happiness.
But think what it means to have composed
a work that later, ages later, bears witness
to the justice of conquest, having praised
violence with its high language and noble rhythms.
Friends. Till your fields. Tend your vines. Raise
bees and cattle. Celebrate labor and the lives
of ordinary, simple things. If anything survives
me, let it be my love of land and boys. I have lit
up the sky with a poem that strikes men blindingly. Burn it.

Caryatids

Shell-white sea-crests pound craggy cliffs
encrusted with impasto thick guano.
Blowing through crevasses in asphalt-
black boulders, over slick glassy slates
of dawn-mirroring rocks, wind-gusts
howl and yip like ululating women
celebrating a city's victory over armies.
Lime-white, flat houses with silvery-
blue shutters peer over a sea where
dolphins play near rot-darkened docks,
now as long before in the old epic stories.

Once it's begun, no despair's ever done.
A herder watches black clouds fade
to a gray like worn linen, torn yet
soft, wispily vanishing into the blue
clarity of more peaceful days, no new
storms soon. He's died here many
times already, broken into fragments,
a shard, a bead, a stoneless ring buried
in sand, tangled in the roots of plane
trees. The sea's will is eternity's will,
he its messenger, the singer of its music.

Each day, he waits patiently by it to die.
It's summer, the island parched by
searing heat. Cicadas rasp, drone
in leaves, among artichoke flowers,
under grasses, sawing, scratching, buzzing,
as night's last gloomy cast cascades

into the sea like a waterfall spraying
gaudy bauble-like bubbles that as a child,
he'd try to grasp hold of. Dawn's light. The wonder
of time is its ease with itself, mornings like temples
capturing each sunrise enraptured by its noble fluted columns.

The Inheritance

1. Central Park

A sweet spring breeze wafts from river to river.
The park's quiet save for a couple of runners.
The sun's stubbornly wintry, white and chilly,
the sky like a satin sheet, blue, flat,
and glossy. When did it begin, this worldly
beauty, profusely given to wind and water?
Only a few taxis roam Manhattan's streets.
On a leash, a dog's sniffing a wall. A rat
pokes its snout out of a trash bin. Mortality
may be the reason that despite what little we see
in life it still amazes us with its feats
of our simply being here among it, mute, dear,
precious, even if meaning nothing much: that knit
mitten in a gutter, that iridescently blue feather
glued to a leaf, that hansom cab's lost leathery horse's bit.

2. Coney Island

Late moonlight glares ice-clear off Coney Island
White water trails behind a trolling boat,
shaping waves into a V. Nothing's planned.
Grebes cry. A line of loose buoys float
past us. Two nearly naked lovers dote
on each other. Restless geese beat gray
wings toward sunrise. The stars appear
to be punctures in the sky's black page
pin-pricked to blank white dots. A cargo-
laden freighter is bound east towards day,
too. Sometimes the world looks like a play,

all artifice, endless movement, night fading near,
then far away. Years ago, here, amazingly, we saw
the Northern Lights and felt a sense of wonder, awe
at how they changed us as they flamed, swirled, and glowed.

3. *Williamsburg and Queensboro Bridges*

Some lights illuminate earth beyond the passing hours
of our human time, the world unpredictable, a many
colored coat, stores' windows, high-rises' towers,
tile roofs, townhouses' marble façades, the glossy
shine after storms resounding off cars, cabs, people's
clothes, signs, billboards, posters, gushing gutters
splashed by trucks, all chromatic mysteries, golden,
silvery, orange, red, green, yellow, purple,
blue while the sun, blurred, half hidden by mist
or fog, shines on the full majesty of Manhattan's
steel bridges so their decks, pylons, cables,
might glow, shimmer, tremble, hesitate. It's like a tryst,
in a way, steel and sunlight uniting like two lovers,
intoxicated, radiant, rapt with desire for each
other, matter, fire, neither reality able to say which is which.

4. *Yorkville*

Years after your death, Manhattan remains the place
for us to meet, no longer having to search
unfamiliar streets for each other. Your face
is mine now, as we sit in a pew in Immanuel Church
near where you were born, eat lunch in a deli,

potato salad, corned beef piled high on sour rye,
ride to Oma's farm on the Staten Island ferry,
devour ice cream on slices of apple pie
at Schroeder's, silently stroll in Schurz Park.
Here, Father, is where, despite the dark
of our pasts, we can greet each other as friends
in that intimacy, that exchange of identity
shared histories offer us, how memory never ends
with us but lives on in the things we die longing to see,
again, roaming your old haunts together, unseen to the city.

5. *Battery Park*

From his Columbia Heights room, Hart watches the bridge
as its spans unfurl like sails, its lights beacons
to faraway lands, offering him passage
to his dreams of Atlantis. He envisions crews, sons
of the sea on a ship that he might embark
on any day now. It's midnight. He's drunk. Stars
play on waves as words do, on winter's ice as
poems do, wildly dancing. Shadows in dark
places lit by streetlights rise and fall like tides.
The bridge lifts its cables hungrily to a silvery
moon. He wonders if this is what it means to pray:
to belong to devotion, to light, to God, to the sea,
to be always dissatisfied. Where he now resides
is no home but a vow, the Battery an unknown shore
where he voyages nightly, cruising the harbor's docks for sailors.

6. *A Playground at Twelfth Avenue*

It's a chilly March morning. A yelping mutt races

past, his paws pulpy messes pressing bright

red prints onto the pavement. As the boy dashes

into traffic, a car's tires screech. The light

changes, but the boy's lost him, tracing

his bloody tracks to a frantic circle he breaks

out of to disappear at the docks, by the rising

river. A tug's horn groans. It takes

his breath away with its mournfulness. He

turns back to Twelfth Avenue, cuts across

an asphalt playground where two kids slowly

rock on a teeter-totter. A third twists her swing's

chains and laughs as she twirls. What is this loss

he feels for a dog whose suffering is all he can imagine

about it? Radio static seeps through a transom. The girl sings and sings.

7. *Three Museums*

He roams through rooms astonished by abstractions the size

of tapestries. MOMA's quiet, no one there to bother

him until a young guard, staring into his eyes

as the boy contemplates a Rothko redder

than red washed with swashes of white, asks

him, "Why do you look so dazzled?" At the Met,

Pollock's "Autumn Rhythm" dares him to risk

expanding into a universal dance that'd let

him dance to earth's pulse. At the Museum of Natural
History, he studies a floor-long stuffed blue whale
dangling from the ceiling, ants entombed in amber,
stars revolving on a planetarium dome, the planet
he lives on's resurrected mesozoic bones. A wintry
light, a silvery air gleams throughout the park where he wanders
after, wondering why there's a world at all, what it means to see it.

8. Times Square

Shrill marquees, flickering bulbs, neon signs,
streetlights, cop cars flashing,
a fat moon trapped between building
and billboard, crowds, long lines
of guys outside a bar, its door
red velvet drapes a few peek
through to see the packed bar,
the filled tables, smell the reek
of booze and smoke thicker
than fog, bored strippers
spotlit by a floodlight
that paints everyone a fiery
blue brighter than the sky
is at noon as the girls dance, grind
against poles, eyes closed, neon lit, light-blinded.

9. Mahler's Sixth at Carnegie Hall

He walks out of the concert hall into a blizzard,
misses his bus' stop at Forty Third,
enters the wrong subway. It's hard
to know where to go, what he's just heard

confusing, scaring him. He climbs
back up, takes a right turn instead
of left, confused by snow. What time
is it now? He can't see. His head
hurts in the icy gusts. Night's music
pursues him, tires grinding through slush,
streetlights buzzing, winds, in a manic
rush, shifting crosstown from hushed
to howling, billboards rattling, alleyways
whistling, cabs clashing until it grows as silent
as after the last hammer blow in the Mahler, fated, yet hesitant.

10. *Second Avenue and 52nd Street*

A pastry shop, its bright green awnings, signs with yellow
scripted lettering, sugar buns sparkling in the window.
Honking cars, taxis. Pounding jackhammers
at two corners, foremen barking orders,
workmen yelling jokes, cursing back and forth.
People racing past each other. What truths
can you see in faces, some blank, stolid, others
joyous or dour, cheerful or sorrowing? The city's
dawn-lit glare casts shadows off its high rises,
poles, billboards, wires. A few blue strewn ribbons
float in the wind. Why? Swallows, swifts, pigeons
fly among them, free as dancers. Noon's light gleams,
outlines, solidifies the forms of passing things. Dreams
are like that, cities, too, their changing patterns breaking open
the beauties sequestered in things, the fantasies, promises you'd forgotten.

11. *Broadway*

They're standing outside the lobby
when his father spots the star,
Alfred Drake, racing swiftly
past them to the stage door,
wearing ascot, goatee, salaaming to
the crowd. Well-dressed ladies
shake change-filled cylinders for
donating coins or bills to benefit
vets, wounded men. One or two
are wearing furs. The show he'll see
is Kismet. Fate. It's eight years after the war.
Strangers with no paradise. "It's all a scam,"
his father informs him as his family sits,
waiting for the music. "They're frauds, cheaters, damn
them," he swears, angrily squeezing his son's clasped hand.

12. *The Cloisters*

A soldier strolls on the walk while his mother
gazes over to the Palisades, the bridge's
towers. Inside, monks start to gather
among wood icons and faded tapestries.
Jesus' face in a crucifix is pocked by
worm holes, the cross partly splintered.
His mother bows to a gold relic holder,
no longer displaying bones, brightly polished.
The stained glass windows paint his hands
and arms green and red. Outside, in
the garden, the air's fresh, herb-scented.
They rest on a bench as the monks begin
to chant. He must be good. Who ever understands
their childhood later? His mother will die and so will he.
The monks' voices rise and fall in arches over the quiet holy city.

Robert Mapplethorpe on Film

The Mineshaft. Westside docks. Raunch bars.
Trucks in the Meatpacking District. Under
the elevated West Side highway. Leather
masks, butt-free pants, plastic suits.
Chains. Racks. Bodies garbed in whatever
clothes, costumes it seeks to make it
shoot, stripped bare, desire intensified
by the role art plays in how a man is fucked
or fucks, in its passion for rites and rituals.

Black is his color, blacker than caves, coal
pits, sludge and slag, sea's abysmal
depths, death's erasures to shut eyes.
Ecstasy. Rapture. No more him, you,
me. Cruising for tricks. Jerking horn-hard
dicks. No Eakins' naked boys on rocks,
overlooking a lake, the lens left open
for a longer exposure of the pastoral scene
as the water's surface breaks. No sentimentality.

Just ardency, men's moans, screams while
ejaculating, snapped, formalized by the click
of a camera, seized in the moment
by the caressing eye of art, the gorgeous
cruelties of anemones, calla lilies,
parrot tulips, orchid and leaf in a white
ovoid vase, their outré faces. Who takes
death's part makes love to its hot beauties.
No white can burn more blindingly than a flash bulb.

A head floats above a carved skull on the tip
of a cane a papery, bony right hand grips.
The background's a blank, painful, lethal
black that's like a white sufficient to appall.
"I'm scared," he cried, dying. And that was it, that was all.

My Father Dying in His Sleep

Snow falling, drayhorses clopping on
cobblestones, ice shards clogging
the East River, skates hanging
from a hook, the rink in Central
Park waiting for him to wake up.

Oma furrows her face as she
smiles at him, her white hair
knotted into a bun, dressed
warmly as they ride the ferry
back to her Staten Island farm.

His mother's eyes glow as she
reads to him in bed, silhouettes
on the ceiling, shadows on
the rug, red roses in papered
walls flickering by gaslit lamps.

Twirling a cane, wearing a cape,
top hat, white gloves, his uncle
greets him at the stage door
of the theater where he'll watch
him act while hidden in the wings.

What is dying to a man ninety
years far from boyhood?
An icy Hudson flowing into
the harbor, tugboats rocking
dockside, ship horn's music,

foghorns groaning as passengers
departing wave back to those
staying, a captain checking
their tickets in his passengers'
log for stowaways on the voyage.

He's leaving Schurz Park, the river,
Jersey shore, farm, Oma, mother,
uncle, the drug store with
the Christmas candy it gave
away, his sister's hand gripping

his as they hide in an alley off
Second Avenue behind thrown-
away crates, playing tag
near a deli smelling of
pastrami, the taste of egg cream

with buddies as sleet returns in
April to freeze Manhattan
before melting into the river,
flowing toward the cold Atlantic
he swam on a dare when seven,

high wood piles in Oma's barn, hay
stacks in the loft, he, his cousins
played in in summer or when
truant from school, new jacket,
long pants, his rushing out

wearing them to show off to
his girlfriend, now twelve like him,
no streetlight in the window, no
city sirens to wake him from
the good boyhood he'd recalled to me

in the nursing home I'd just moved
him to, condemned there for
the sin of aspiration, two hours
before he died in his sleep in memory's
dream-like care, I pray, its lingering traces of grace.

Virgin Forest

The young sky's the faded blue and white
of antique porcelain. The air shimmers
to the sound of cow and church bells far
away. Boxwood hedges, yellow,
purple irises garland a pond
smelling sweetly of must, woody
and redolent. With a spring flare
to them, wild roses bloom more freely
left unseen, like new shoots rising out
of rain-softened ground showing off
their innocence to no one but themselves.

Wolf spiders, Parson spiders, milkweed stalks,
lilies by a creek, sun-inspired odors
of magnolia, gardenia thickening air
like a rainy day, petals spiraling down,
no fences, walls, only green ferns,
grass to rest on, spicy spruce
needles, resinous chips of pine bark:
the green world he's failed stays
real, however imaginary his childhood's
self-exile into unmapped wilderness, dream-
like and dangerous, heartless in its peacefulness,

Its fresh leaves sparkling, winged seeds,
elated by morning's breezes, drifting,
white, silvery threads of dandelion,
dew, silvery mist unsubdued by dawn's
hazy light, alighting on vines, ivy,

wind-blown petals yielding to earthly
slumber. So legends began of lost girls
and boys never to be called home
again, having fallen asleep as children
will do, exhausted after a long day's playing,
as he is, deep in the woods of the good and blessed,

children who've waited for twilight, flocks of swallows
swirling like whirlwinds, clouds of ash
and dust hurtling through the sky,
geese flying northward as if to meet
their shadows arriving before them. It's time
to gather sunless flowers closing its petals,
to drink of a meadow's icy springs, you
who were young once, lolling under the shades
of ash and elm, listening to the susurrus
of breezes' ghostly murmurings welcoming
you into the freedom from time in a virgin forest.

How hushed, hesitant it is. The moon obliquely
lights his way toward a new dwelling place,
guided by a kingfisher's feathers, its sunset-
lit golden breast. Clouds pour out of its
mountains with no place to settle
once winter's started, the last crimson
leaves searing the limbs of maple, oak,
hickories as thoughts of lost things turn
to tears, chilling an aged heart on a darkening
evening, till he falls asleep, till he falls asleep
to willows' catkins blossoming, partridges flying overhead.

Mercy, Bringer of Rain

A dry river, its rocky, weed-
infested shallows,
paddy fields
dying, flowers gone to seed,
ploughs
rusting, what wields
this power? A bluestone
buddha, eyes closed,
meditating alone,
a chiseled, polished
smile on its face in consolation
as a sapphire-feathered martin
flies overhead, the moon rising
like a lantern approaching
closer, like a dog, wary of fire,
holding back, sniffing,
like a man uncertain of his future.

Coarse winds foul swallows'
wings. Stars tire
of their colors, flowers
sputter like candles. Town
after town dreams
of flowing streams,
of jade beds, down
pillows,
of winnowing
wheat, tomorrows
better than yesterdays, listening for thunder
to rumble, for the first lightning crack, boulder,

bellbine, rhododendron,
snakeroot, mountain
springs, valley meadows all waiting for rain,
the fluent words of the prayed for mortal consolation
of this land, these rivers.

August in Carolina, 1955

1.
Two curing barns, unpicked persimmons
rotting on slick, glazed, wet red
clay, the sun golden as the thin

small cross necklace my mother wears
to church, a shingle and slate
roofed, weathered, hive-colored

farm house, cardboard plugging holes
in two cracked windows, three
pair of faded jeans dangling

from a clothesline, flapping in the wind
next to five t-shirts, and a half-
dozen saggy briefs,

a tractor with wheels tall as Cliff
is, deep in a ravine,
doves warbling in cadences

like his voice as he sings softly
while working in the tobacco
fields as I listen,

hiding in nearby woods, not like a spy
but in the spirit
of defiance.

2.
Near the edges of a water pump,
weeds thrive from years
of overspill's flowing

like rivulets formed after summer
showers. His brothers, father
nap in a cooling shade

or share the jug of iced water Cliff offers
as brown reeds, withered from
weeks of heat, rustle in dry breezes.

3.
After August thunderstorms, the earth
steams like boiling water—
even at night, too hot

to sleep in as everyone waits
for the moon to rise
with a promise of cooler skies,

the air in day's still simmering
aftermath smelling
like seared metal.

As crickets prolong their chirruping,
moonlight falls
on the sweltering earth

softly as white rhododendron petals
or slips of torn paper swirling
in cooling gusts.

4.

On a bare barrel, its hoops rusty,
a crow cracks acorns
as a scraggly black cat

prepares to pounce on it
until the buzz and rasp
of locusts

rise like a warning to frighten
the bird away, soaring
off on a blistering sky-seeking current.

5.

I learned back home how compassion
can be discerned in how,
as a small rat gnaws

futilely at a discarded jam jar,
a rush of wind can come
to topple it to pieces on a brick floor.

6.

As a rare chill morning hints of autumn,
crickets chirrup more quietly
while dozens of butterflies

dart in and and out of rose bushes
and honeysuckle vines
as if they were half aware

of how little time was left them.
Dew drops sparkle on
spiders' webs, their patterns

intricate as a child's kaleidoscope
or the waves formed in
a pond as two boys toss rocks into it.

7.

A crescent moon vanishes from the sky
at daybreak, morning heat
swiftly following,

Cliff sleeping next to me smelling of pine
trees made even more
resinous when first light's blazing sun's

consummates its nostalgic bond to
the earth, we two sticky
and sweaty, lovers of summer,

lying on yellowed sheets,
wet from our bodies,
together for the first and last time.

8.

In a far away dream of summer,
green trees offer
shade all day,

like a stone temple mirrored
in a lake where gentle
bursts of wind

ripple the water and scents
of roses blossoming
everywhere.

I am grown tired from age,
remembering a white
swirl of cooling

clouds whirling like a tornado
out of the eastern horizon,
then darkening,

bringing lightning as I sit on
a rock wall,
lolling, idling, waiting

for the musky, pine-scented winds
of a Southern summer
thunderstorm

to cool the earth of its searing August
heat, watching a crow
perching on a scarecrow,

ruffling its feathers, flying off
towards clouds
grown black as it is,

and later among the hazy blackness of pines,
I'd walk under moonlight,
the bright moon

and the shadow of pine, and think of him
as I do now, working the fields
with his brothers

unceasingly in the storm, the rain falling gray
as charcoal dust,
continuing late into evening,

and I slowly, even now, coming to know at last
this earth is my love,
my passion.

Eight Love Sonnets for Atticus Carr

1.

In the Asian Museum each visit, we'd study

the cloisonné butterflies and scarlet finches
stitched like light on a gown and the sea
in a scroll beside it painted as if a breeze
were softly wafting over the water while
clouds bathed the coast in sun-rise gold.
You grasped my hand and fell silent, a smile
broadening on your face as you looked that told
more surely than words could of your happiness
at being alive in this world and led me to remember
your gift of two dozen or more stargazer lilies
that seemed to be luminescent in their darker-
than-night porcelain vase, emitting a scent so tellingly
sweet it filled the room with your love and all it forgives in me

2.

At mere sight of you, Sappho wrote, my voice
falters, my tongue is broken The mist is sun-lit
this morning, the Pacific mottled, sod-green,
streaked with yellow, strewn with seaweed it
tossed on the beach last night. So I've seen
it for many years now. For how much longer, the choice
is not mine to make. Robbie's snout rests on
your thigh as you drowse. Despite the light shining
outside curtained windows, our house remains
dark until we open the draperies to a late sun
that won't fade books, CD cases, photographs, paintings.

The pleasures that pass between us each night gain
more meaning as we grow older. You are still reading
your book as I walk our dog, the air chill, salty, and comforting.

3.

At the Asian Museum, we read the legend about how
the crane of the heart flies toward the sun
to burn illusions away. Below it, the doors of the House
of Pleasure always stay open. Below it, streams still run
toward a river where they flow in a common course
toward the sea. Two men sit by a quiet lake, their row
boat tied to a dock and recall a night together
when they drank wine until there was no more left to drink
and drunkenly watched by lantern light the fishes glitter
like starlight in the lake where they saw—maybe still think
they can see—two cranes stalking through reeds, churning
the water, waves rippling toward the sandy bank where, getting
sleepy, the men rested until, as day broke, the birds took flight,
sunward, not two birds, but one free of illusions, soaring out of sight.

4.

He tugs out weeds, prunes bushy plants growing
too high, puts in new sod and fertilizer, tills
the soil, waters flowers, humming, smiling
like a child playing a game with trolls,
imagining them alive with tales to tell.
Everywhere in the small yard, gophers dig holes,
eat roots, destroy what they devour, yet dwell
safely underground. It's an endless battle
between him and them they win since he's incapable

of harming a soul. Romance errs when it compares love to
flowers, beautiful and evanescent. What of the one who
tends them daily, watches over, worries about them?
Maybe gardening is his lapsed Catholic way of singing hymns
as he cares for nemesia, salvia, oxalis, peonies, marigolds, mums.

5.

Elusive silence, the mutely meaningful thing
I have tried to hear in the music I
listen to, not what a singer might sing
or an orchestra play but what might lie
silent in the notes, hidden, not sounded
but implied, like a word never said
but spoken anyway, understood yet a mystery,
like someone seen from afar or by failing eyes.
I've told you how I once saw in a rose stem
broken by sunlight in its crystal vase an image
as lovely and calm and wise as an ancient sage,
like a Buddha almost, or as a crèche from Bethlehem
I could believe in as I did long ago, as I believe in love
when it's left untold like anything too important to speak of.

6.

Last night, we embraced as the young do, not
asking more from time than it is willing to give
us, not expecting another July 4th on a hot
night on China Beach, firecrackers, like live
ammunition, exploding around us that gave
new meaning to the holiday as we made love in
a cliffside cave. How long can memories save

us, or shouldn't we ask them to? Are words that begin
in the past able to endure a lifetime? Note them down
in your heart like images from a poem you love so
much, have read so often you've memorized it. Brown
thoughts obsess the old. How much there is left to do,
to learn, to know? It may surprise you I speak of God, Emily
Dickinson wrote, who know him but a little, but witchcraft is wiser than we.

7.

At the Asian Museum, we can't see the screen in one view.
No matter how far back we stand, the mountains, like
gigantic moss-covered pine cones, lean, bent askew
by time and weather, its slopes too sheer to hike.
We move from panel to panel. Much is shown in miniature,
minuscule cranes, two men poling two tiny boats
on a river widening where it's fed by streams. Culture
is the past transfigured into stories. A solitary duck floats
on a pond. High up, in a wood hut, two aged men
wearing fluent robes talk while gesturing, their faces
little more than a few quick brush strokes. In a den,
or maybe it's the open mouth of a cave, a monk
sits, contemplating the grace of clouds and a plum tree trunk,
knowing, like the begging bowl he holds, heaven is everywhere he gazes.

8.

A small dog, a brindled poodle mix, lies in the north-bound
lane of The Great Highway, run over or hit.
Cars dash past or attempt to drive around
it. If it's not yet dead, it soon will be if it
isn't rescued by someone. Careless of his safety,

Atticus leaps off the walkway into traffic, picks
the dog up, cradles it like a child, and carries it free
from peril. Its tag reveals its name. The dog licks
his cheeks. The woman who runs toward him saw the harms,
risks he'd faced for her dog's sake. He returns it to her arms
as she cries in gratitude. Life turns all into parable. A lost sheep
lies hurt in a thicket among brambles and briars in great danger
of dying from wolves and foxes. A man passes by who'd give his all
to save it, even his life. Say he's not a shepherd, but one who follows his call.
That is love.

Peter Weltner lives in San Francisco by the Pacific and its new park, Sunset Dunes, with his partner, Atticus Carr. His previous books include, in fiction, The Risk of His Music, How the Body Prays (both Graywolf Press), and The Return of What's Been Lost (Marrowstone); in poetry, Vespers on Point Reyes: Selected Poems (BrickHouse Books), Crow-Black Stones and a Flock of Crows (Agenda Editions, UK), and Water's Eye, Bird and Tree/In Place, Woods and the City, After, Old-Songs Re-played, and The Lost Ghosts of Lemnos (all Marrowstone).

I wish to give a deep bow of gratitude for their words about my work to Susan Crowl, Forrest Gander, Clarinda Harriss, editor emerita of BrickHouse Books, Patricia McCarthy, editor emerita of Agenda, Nancy McDermid, Jonathan Middlebrook, Robert Mohr, David Morris, William O'Daly, Galen Williams, Jason Wirth, Nathan Wirth, and Lindley Young.

And for all they have given me in the past, and still wonderfully do, I want to thank the late Stephen Arkin, Gerald Coble, Robert Colley, and Sam Crowl. But above all this book is my inadequate offering in thanks-giving for the love of my husband of forty years, Atticus Carr.